Poetry In a Pohutukawa

Poetry In a Pohutukawa

REGGIE REFLECTIONS

R. de Wolf

Rhythmic Weave Books

Published by Rhythmic Weave Books
An Imprint of R. de Wolf
PO Box 438
Gisborne 4040
Email: rdewolfngarimu@gmail.com
www.rdewolf.com

ISBN: 978-1-99-118961-5 Softcover

A catalogue record for this book is available from the National Library of New Zealand

Cover Art by Regina de Wolf-Ngarimu
Rhythmic Weave Logo credit www.vecteezy.com/free-vector/ornament Ornament Vectors by Vecteezy

First Printing, 2022

Printed in Australia

Dedication

In loving memory

of

Mum - Lydia Dawn Ngarimu
&
Friend - Ella Moray Williams

Who twinkle above
Bathing us in starlight
And, aroha (love) forever.

Books & Stories by R. de Wolf

Guardians of the Ancestors
Book One of the Spirit Voyager Series

The Future Weavers
Book Two of the Spirit Voyager Series

Poetry In a Pear Tree
An accessible book of poetry for anyone

The Goodness Algorithm
Evolutionary Dystopia

Brothers in Whalesong
Book Three of the Spirit Voyager Series

Short Stories in Anthology
Kaituhi Rāwhiti - A Celebration of East Coast Writers
Crushed Violet
Kaituhi Rāwhiti Two - Weaving of Words
Whale Brothers
The Hollow Mother

Contents

Contents - *xi*

Kina Killer

Touch me if you dare!

Thorny spines stain hunters' fingers
If you want me – suffer
Spikes through sugar bag, pierce back

Split of knife
Scrape of teaspoon
Precious roe
Untangled from guts
Put it in the container?

Magnetised to mouth
Salty, sweet, umami
Flavour of the sea

Creamy summer dreaming
Slurping gifts of Tangaroa
Salivating, hand too slow

Empty, shell-piled roasting dish – oops!

Morena sunshine!
Toxic tent
Salty treats demand fluid chasers

Sweet revenge on guts – kina.

***Slurping Scribe** confesses her love for kina - sea urchin. A tastebud crush that developed early and has withstood the tick of time to blossom into an enduring love. Alas, for the scribe, but lucky for the kina, the writer is no 'kina hunter'.

When the scribe was a kid, at the beach with Nanny Maraea, they could find kina in the rockpools to fill their kete, and just took enough for a feed. Those days are gone and now you need to be a good diver. While the scribe can snorkel and scuba dive, she swims like a rock that loves the seabed and the water is too cold for her.

So, the scribe is content with her role at the dish, pretending to poha (remove the roe from the shell), while she eats.

Happily, sister Kerry keeps her company. Everyone rolls their eyes at them because they know why they're there and try to poha faster than they can eat - good luck with that!

Aroha

Thoughtful care, giving
Selfless consideration
to others gifted
Compassionately mindful
Sharing, exposed naked heart

*Optimistic Romantic Raver, realised she included Aroha in Poetry In a Pear Tree, but somehow it got a bit lost, so here it shall remain at the beginning of this book. Many words, lines, poems and books have been written about love - still, we don't understand it or the effects love can wield.

Romantic love is the craziest basketcase on the block, with no rhyme, or reason for the dramatic reactions of our hormones or the chemicals our bodies make. In a logical world, we would fall for the perfect match that is good for us. In the real world, parents everywhere shake their heads and emit loud sighs because they knew their child's relationship was doomed from day dot. But, love is unpredictable and sometimes survives the craziest of times. 'There is always hope,' said an old guy with a long beard.

Purple

Oozy well
Purple hazed inkpot
Tart acidity
Swirl of plummy pleasure

Flirtatious tastebuds
Crystalline geometry of teeth
Compressed rock
Taniwha spine of amethyst

Grapes gasping
Demanding attention
Languishing in my glass
Enticing, to taste their purpality

Lavender laced perfume
Dancing
In Aunty's handkerchief
Potpourri ambush in drawer

I am purple
Unabashed aubergine
I am different
Velvet depth of pansy-purpleness

Am I 'purplier' than others?
No, but my myriad shades colour the world
Uniquely organic
Proudly purple

*A poem that started out as wordplay and homage to the delicious richness of everything purple. Then my Taniwha popped into the text to create depth to the purpality. Do we celebrate our uniqueness as often as we should? Are we teaching our rangatahi, and living the example that says, 'hey it's ok to be different' or 'just be you, I love you as you are'? Like light refracted from the crystalline faces of an amethyst, Purple invokes unique meaning to bespoke humans - churr.

Rehua & Matariki

A CELESTIAL LOVE STORY

Aeons pass
Quiet contemplation abounds
Heaven-nestled whare
Te Matau a Maui – Scorpius to some

Gaze-raked universe
Cloudy galaxies spiral, expand, contract
Asteroids collide
Stars glitter, majestic in transformation

Minerals disperse – oh! spectacular display
Planets and moons slide in orbit
Binary stars dance well-rehearsed steps
What more is there, for Atua?

Rehua spies Matariki
Wreathed, in distant celestial glory
Once seen
Unforgettable visions haunt dreams

Heavens wheel
Perpetual movement of existence
But Rehua is transfixed
Magnetised by Matariki

Lightning-bolts flare
Inspiration to action
Harnessing cosmic energy
Rehua leaps astride prancing comet

Blazing through constellations
Spurring on celestial steed
Rocketing onward, closer
Beacon shimmering - Matariki

Sheen of twilit hair
Tendriled in magnificence
Entwining beams
Woven through starlight cloak

They regard one another
Rehua and Matariki
Star, embracing manuhiri
Atua and whetu – together at last

The magic of meeting
Banished aloneness
Star-shot bursts of ecstasy

Heavens erupt - divine love

Explosive birthing
Fusion of fission
Fuelling creation - explosive brood
Golding the universe

Whaea – Rehua sighs
Tamariki to guide life, Matariki smiles
Whanau, yours and mine Rehua
Constellation of purpose

With their grandparents
Sparkling newborns
Are showered in gifts
Each one, twinkling significance

They can't live together
Forever, Whetu and Atua
But, across the cosmos
Worship each other from afar

Proud parents
Stars born in aroha
Bathed in the guiding quicksilver
Of Rehua and Matariki.

Footnote for the Curious:
Are there seven?

Or nine?

Fourteen or hundreds?

The passions of Matariki, are private & confidential.

*Starstruck Storyteller - Told or typed, the love story was invented long before Shakespeare, Barrett Browning or Neruda dipped their quills to ink and shaped words that would be spoken for years untold. If we peer back in time, the abundance of material available is simply mind-blowing. The Egyptians, Persians, Chinese, Greeks, Romans, Japanese - too many to name - produced incredible oral and written tales to tantalise, entertain and capture historic events. The writer looked closer to home for this poem, but gazed back into the mists of time and creation.

Rehua and Matariki was initially a writing project to celebrate Matariki and coincided with the first Public Holiday in Aotearoa in 2022, recognising the Maori New Year. The poet aired the offering on stage at the wonderful Matariki Arts Festival in Te Tairawhiti, alongside talented artists from the Tai Tech Writing Group. But, as poetry does, this piece is comprised of many layers of meaning and inspiration. Some of it was instigated by the retelling of a Maori story by Katrina Reedy, while other components incorporate the korero and stargazing on an Astro Tour with John Drummond. It's also an inter-entity, non-binary love match - do we need a gender box for our stars and Gods or at all really?

Aroha - love knows no boundaries and transcends the comprehension of mere mortals.

Taonga

Intangible
Yet often lost
Missed without acknowledgment

    Precious
    But taken for granted
    Shared dish – not always passed

        Taonga
        Worth recognised
        Treasured, handed, generation to generation

            Knowledge
            Intangible, precious, taonga
            Rejoice in the preservation of wisdom.

*Literary Lament - to the cultural knowledge lost when it isn't passed on. Whether it's repeating stories orally, working together on craft, making a video, or writing a book, we are all walking talking repositories of information. How and what, will our relatives of the future know of us in generations to come? There was a time when we all lived more traditionally, working together every day, and learning the family skills to survive. What will you leave behind for those who will follow?

Lydia Dawn

Born on sea-fringed shore
Wharekauri
Into arms of William and Cassie Grennell
Sister of Joy and Joe

Horse saddled
School bus
Cantering off
Pulling cousin Alma aboard

Alas, William departed too soon
The winds of Wharekauri
Blew Cassie and whanau
To Te Waipounamu

Tuahiwi marae
Step-Dad Uncle Bruce
Rangiora High
Awaited

Wellington beckoned

Off you went to study nursing
Not to be your cup of tea
Better to become a secretary

But Alma called for you
"Come Lydia, to the East Coast, visit me"
Stay with the Goldsmith's
Across the Waiapu

Rain came
Flooding changed and shaped lives
You met a man, your love
Husband and father to be

Wedding planner for Alma
Pine came courting
And your married
At Pohatukura

Whareponga living
Farmer's wife
Horsewoman
Truck driver

Baking
Brawn making
Mincing and preserving fruit
Raising children

Taught them to read

Indulged curiosity
Filled lunchboxes
On a skinny budget

Thrifty
Inventive and resilient
Strong
Constant

Quietly doing everything
That needed to be done
You loved
And were loved in return

What an accomplished woman
You were Lydia
Seamstress
Librarian

Nanny
So many mokopuna
Even more great-grandchildren
And one great great

Wife
Pine's wife
Lydia Dawn Grennell – Pomare
Lydia Dawn Ngarimu – Mum.

*Literary Love - I loved my Mum as most people who are lucky enough to be nurtured by a mother do. She pushed five of us out into the world, fed, clothed, shooed us off to school, loved us, and growled when we needed some discipline. It was a privilege to have parents who stayed with us so long - Dad was 79 and Mum was a month away from being 89.

My lake of tears is for myself. I know Mum couldn't wait to be with Dad, in heaven, by his side where she always wanted to be. Mum gifted us a connection to Rekohu - Wharekauri - The Chatham Islands, and to Te Waipounamu through our Nana and America and England through her Dad. Most of all, we treasure our whanau from Mum's side of the tree, even though we don't see each other often. Right little cocktails we are, although we always identify ourselves as Maori, because Dad was Ngati Porou and Te Whanau-a-Apanui - a self-proclaimed Hori (he wore this description with pride) and a Coastie through and through. They are probably still celebrating East Coast Rugby up there this year.

In my heart, in my soul, and in my DNA, everything I write reminds me what good parents we had - not perfect, not TV parents but our parents.

Cardigan

A name of Welsh origin
An 'Englishing' of Ceredigion or "Ceredig's land"
This chap, or lass who knows, Ceredig,
Roamed rolling Welsh hills in the 5th Century

Our prissy little garment
Convenient and oft buttoned
Is credited to James Brudenell
The 7th Earl of Cardigan

I am amused to envision
This British Major General
Leading the Charge of the Light Brigade
Knitting needles tucked safely in his cardie

Did he dream of plain and purl?
While fighting at Balaclava
Cardigan born of officers knitted wool waistcoat
Fashionable in the 1800s

So our dear sweet cardigan, bears the Earl's name

But I suspect, somewhere unknown in a corner
Needles clattered, while women chattered
And that is how the cardigan was actually made

I doubt the sandwich was made by the Earl
Who never entered a kitchen
But by some clever maid, who invented what he liked
To stop his picking and finicky bitchin'

And as for the Earl we hear every day
Who never tread land or saw our lovely city
Please take your Lion's feet, off our waka
Colonial brand, cultural divide - such a pity

So now when weather or breeze turns cool
And I reach for my trusty cardie
At least I'm more informed of Earls
Their cooking, knitting, and naming parties.

*Aristocastic Author - what a prompt cardigan turned out to be. Off the author scurried to research the origins of said cardie. Of course, like most English words, its origins lay elsewhere - Wales and Welsh. Credited to a man who probably wouldn't know a knitting needle if he sat on it. I mean really, was the 7th Earl sitting in his tent knitting? The thought of it led me to other Earls credited with inventing stuff or having places named after them - ridiculous! Some unknown woman knitted the cardigan, the same as somebody in the kitchen invented the sandwich and as for Gisborne he never came to Aotearoa.

Besides 'Gisborne' already had and has a name Turanganui-a-Kiwa and there have never been lions in New Zealand. So, how that crazy crest with lion's paws standing on Horouta came to be, we can only attribute to .... you choose the word/s.

If you ask your mokopuna about the cardie, you will get a mostly enthusiastic "Wow! I didn't know you even liked Cardi B!" Aka Belcalis Marlenis Almanzar, the famous American Rapper.

The author's decree - 'Earl's should stick to their knitting.'

Did the author mention her name means Queen in Italian and Latin?

Remembered

Soldiers neath earth
Living, invisibly scarred
Battling for freedom

Sorrow soaked landscapes
Littered field, war-shattered dreams
Lamenting lost loves

Now, remembering
Cold, eternal
Gift of youth

Sacrifice, for us.

*There can never be enough words written to honour our fallen soldiers. War touches us all, and tears are never far away. Lest we forget.

Tree

Falling, flying, wind-tugged seed
Sneeze-tossed by Tawhirimatea

Playful tumbling of life-blessed hope
Falling, dropping, gravity pulled seed

Papatuanuku clasping to breast
Nurtured purchase, self-planted in earth

Growing, slurping, finger-rooted grasp
Matariki influenced, sprouting held fast

Swaying in seasons, moon-stretching reach
Seedling, unfurling, spring-kissed leaf

Clasped tightly to Tane, flesh wrapped bones
Strategically branching, for oft-sought light

Yearning, longing, to tower above
Tane's children, humus-fuelled love

Expanding, twig to trunk, sun-dappled skin
Sprawling behemoth, shade-making friend

Shoots on high, Ranginui beckons, year-measured climb
Brooding, cloaked magnificence, foliage to spend

Passing waters, running time, age-lichened limbs
Longing for, returned affection, Mother awaits

Patiently, feeding, nutrient-given embrace
Raging storm, lightning-sizzle, thunder-split strike

Roiling hills, Ruamoko stomped, root-wrenching might
Creaking, groaning, ground-beat anguish of crash

Seeking, gathering, tender-shooted teen
Craving warmth, gift of Maui, char-licked wood

Turning, smoking, combustion, flame-heated kai
Rising, sparking, arms extended toward sky

Consumed in ravened-maw, voraciously alive
Sighing, curling, wanders tendril-burnt drift

Carbonising, tantalising, ash-cooled remnants aground
Home-coming to Earth Mother, cycle turning profound

Breathing, being, forest-inhaled, tree.

*Papatuanuku Poet - Trees, nature, and mother earth have inspired orators and poets since they came to exist. Our poet chose the life cycle of a tree, and through its stages of life, to pen this homage. They are beauty in our landscapes, shelter from storms, breath of nature, and warmth on cold nights - our life is beautiful because of the tree.

Finding Unicorn

Scratch, scratch, the white
Undercoat, grey to black

Beauty, buried rainbows beneath
I see you, unicorn.

You are here
You walk the streets
No paint can ever erase
That you belong

*Wistful Writer - It's ok to be a minority and proud of it. It's ok to be unusual and unique - there is beauty in diversity. The species hunted almost to extinction, holds a strange fascination, and appreciated value, once it's almost eradicated. There's a place in the world for unicorns, even if they are so very hard to find.

Kumara

TRIBUTE TO RONGO FROM THE FUTURE WEAVERS

Kumara
Unique
Moonlit mishap
Lumpy
Deceptive hidden beauty
Thick-skinned, purple rank
Buried in black
Benign unthreatening
Character starched resolve
Underestimated - the power of kumara
Persuasive, seductive, enduring, endearing
Subterranean sweetness
Underlying ungainly form
Tuber in waiting
Born to nourish
Cultivator of people
Kumara

*Scribbler Softy - Rongo, affectionately nicknamed Kumara, is one of the Scribbler's favourite characters from novel The Future Weavers - Book 2 of the Spirit Voyager Series. Why, you might ask? He is described perfectly in the poem. A humble, unattractive man who is sweet, deadly with a taiaha, smart enough to wield diplomacy, and a cultivator of people. The qualities that lie under the scary exterior, make Rongo an intriguing and complex character. He captures the unwilling heart of his beautiful woman, is loved by his men and children, and even earns the respect of his enemies - no spoilers here!

The skills of Rongo are shared with Marama's sons, Maui and Kai, so Kumara gets a few mentions in Book Three Brothers in Whalesong.

The Riches of Yellow

Yellow house
Yellow car
Welcome home
From afar

For flowers it is
Such a cheerful colour
When it comes to the coating
Could it get any duller

Yes, it's the pollen
I'm talking about
The yellow of sneezes
We could all live without

Getting up our noses
To make rivers of snot
Or irritating eyes
Itching mess till bloodshot

Hayfever sufferers

Who needs to breathe anyway
Competition for gorse
Privet and hay

Wish James Cook watched
A funny landing video
Need to keep our home safe
From invasive pests don't you know

500 million kilograms
Of pollen each year
Clouds of dust announce
Pinus radiata is here

They suck up water
And nutrients, for years on end
To produce a cheap log
For our foreign friends

Do we build any houses?
No - don't be absurd
We pulp the low-grade ones
To wipe the odd turd

Who needs houses
We have yellow, to make our lives merry
A profusion of pollen
Can't make wood it's too scary

Now dear reader

You may detect a cynical tone
Don't worry, no one's listening
Better talk to a stone

For we are content
With our poor little lot
We have pollen and tissues
To catch buckets of snot.

*Pollenhatred Poet - What can the Poet say? The damn pollen tortures her every year with all the above afflictions. Then, to top it all off, the house needs to be water blasted by hubby from top to bottom.

500 million kgs of pine pollen later, we haven't really measured the impact on us or the long-term effect on our whenua - land. There may be some wonderful products that can be created from pine pollen but do we have to cover the whole country with them?

The poet loves trees, pine trees included in moderation - although hacking one down for Christmas is apparently, satisfying revenge. Planting more native trees would make a lot of sense, even though we can't use them to manufacture tissues and toilet paper - they are beautiful and they belong in our landscape.

Diversity is a thing, a good thing, economically, biologically, and environmentally. Poet is hoping we learned a lesson from the sheep fiasco in the 70s - let's not put all our eggs, or pollen, in one basket.

Bobbing for Koura

A story told by Dad when we lived in Waiomatatini
Stoked children's sense of adventure
Rumbled our puku with imagined feeds
Of silky, succulent
Koura

'Take us bobbing' we begged
'First you have to make the tools' Dad said

So off we went in search of chicken wire
Old broom handles and branches
Hammered and nailed, some of them failed
A few thumbs hit
But glowing with pride we announced
'We did it Dad, we are ready'

He sent us in search of fragrant bait
To attract our quarry
While we lay in wait
'The worse it smells, the better it works,' said Dad

What will work best we pondered?
Dog tucker on the turn?
Or a mess of squished up worms?

We settled on possum, road-kill baked
Maggoty, putrid, torture on the nose

At last we piled onto the back of the truck
Not to Whareponga, where we wandered as babes
But off to Tikapa, closer to home

Beach silvered moonlight
Torch flickered white sand
We traipsed round the rocks
Stinky bobs in hand

Disappointed and small, I sat on the rocks
Minding the gear
While whanau dipped bobs in salted pools
Dad held his finger to his lips for quiet
All we had to do, was wait for a torturous time

When the bobs were lifted
Heaved from the water
Covered in koura, clambering for bait
We whooped for joy, so easy to catch

No diving, no glove – why didn't we do this before?
Time scudded past
Clock whizzed

Fun

'Time to go, the tide is coming in' Dad said
He slung our haul, over his shoulder
We skipped over rocks
Chattering madly
Full of stories and debating who caught the most
The biggest koura, the highest number in one go
Released from silence, words tumbled aplenty
'Wait til Mum sees how many we got'
Dad was probably grateful
Kids were on the back of the truck

I suspect I slept on the way home
A night to remember
Night well-lived, now gone

But sometimes I see road-kill possums
And smile
A player in
Bobbing for koura.

*Salivating Scribbler - loves succulent sweet koura served with a side of wasabi memoir mayo. The magic of a moonlit night of adventure with her Dad, Whina, Willie and Kerry is engraved in the 'Book of Awesome.'

Nana's Stone Friend

APOSTROPHE POEM

Tell me, stone, what was it like living in the South Island all those years?

Did you know my Nana? She was born in Te Waipounamu too.

I only met her twice when I was small.

Once she came to visit us in Reporoa, Mum and I flew to Christchurch in 1974 to see her in Woodend.

Now she is buried at Tuahiwi, not so very far from where I picked you up.

You did know her! How lucky you are.

I would have liked to know Nana better.

Was she good at telling stories, and did she give her mokopuna cuddles before bed?

If you speak to her again, stone, I would be grateful if you could tell her a couple of things from me, because when I went to her unveiling, all her other mokopuna from the south adored growing up with her.

I would like you to tell her, "thank you, Nana, for creating all the little parts of me that are you. I wish we had visited and seen you more often."

Do you think she might want to hear about my life stone? That I travelled and worked all over the world, or that I am married and love writing and music.

I would have loved to hear her stories stone.

Like how she met Grandad and ended up living on the Chatham Islands, whether she loved the feel of the wind in her hair and what food she liked to eat, was she happy with her life? Did she have any regrets, or had she accomplished achievements that made her proud.

It was the funniest thing stone when I arrived in Te Waipounamu, I felt the whenua wrap around me, and my tīpuna seemed to drift in the mist and snow.

Somehow Rakiura and Te Whara Whara welcomed me into their arms stone. I wonder if Nana knew of any connections to these magical places.

I'm a little bit envious of you stone because you knew my Nana.

But, she resides in my heart and soul.

You are such a good listener, stone!

I hope I am not boring you.

*Conversation Chronicler - What a fantastic form of poetry

Apostrophe is. The Chronicler isn't sure what it is about speaking to an object that brings thoughts to the surface, which weren't previously perceived. A buried yearning for a grandmother barely known or perhaps a dawning realisation of missing out on a valuable relationship due to distance?

People are fortunate to live in an age of affordable air travel and modern vehicles. The trick is to make the most of the resources and connect with relatives while you can.

Test Tube

Chemically combining
Creating, building,
Inside glass womb
Dividing, multiplying
Multiplying, merging - complex
All of me swirling
Elements, solutions, acids
Chromosomes
Grasping for consciousness
Struggling to be
Hopelessly human
Stretching to survive
Organs growing
Blueprint of genes
Poetry in perfection
I am me
Let me out
Mother test tube
I want to live.

*Pencil-pimped Poet - a prompt that first took the poet catapulting back to the 90s and a club in Potts Point Sydney called the Test Tube Factory. She can still see the neon lights decorating the walls and bar, not to mention those little racks of drinks they nursed back to their lab stools like mad professors.

The result of those experiments? Pretty much the same as other drinks consumed in glasses at other establishments!

Poet happened to be writing her fourth novel, The Goodness Algorithm when Test Tube popped into her life, so she was consumed by the future where babies are genetically screened and grown in a laboratory. Not a novel concept, pardon the pun, but the exploration of what happens when nature is tampered with and humans try to control evolution was foremost in her mind.

Chowder Recipe

1 cup of average
1 cup of ordinary
3 tablespoons of same same
2 leaves of selfish
½ teaspoon of intolerance
A pinch of superiority to taste
1 heaped tablespoon of NIMBY

Combine all ingredients and mix vigorously. Place on high heat and stir continuously, apply blow-torch if necessary, for 200 years until the mixture is hard and inflexible. Be sure to remove any lumps or anomalies to create a silky smooth chowder that will wow you with its blandness.

Alternatively:
6 grinds of black pepper
2 hot chilli people
1 cup of diversity
2 cups of acceptance
3 teaspoons of distilled unicorn tears

5 heaped tablespoons of love
A pinch of flexibility

Simmer slowly, mixing gently and continuously for an unforgettable dish.

*Recipe Writer was inspired by the past of a city far away, but this is an international dish that was, and still is, served in many countries. The hamburger and chips of crappy human behaviour, unfortunately. But I am an eternal optimist who has the pot on simmer for the alternative recipe. When it has bubbled and simmered for long enough, with just the right amount of stirring, the chowder will be sublime. I vote the bland recipe gets thrown out with soup, pot and cooks.

Starman's Story

A SPIRIT VOYAGER PREQUEL

A gem of the Pacific, Starboy's home. Shining white sand, tepid turquoise, lazy palm trees growing coconuts, a tranquil village. The reef teems with colour, life, and delicious fish. In deep water, grains of sand wrap themselves layer upon layer, patiently transforming into lustrous pearls.

He squinted as a strange waka hove into view. Warriors came ashore, greeted by the grown-ups, offered food and water. Starboy continued his search for crabs, a favourite food for his family.

The strangers shared a generous evening meal, enchanted by the hula dancers' fluid hips, riveted by the physical beauty of the women. They glimpsed paradise, with the covetous hearts of raiders, as they weighed precious pearls for trade.

Faint light before dawn cracked the darkness. Starboy jerked awake. Movement all around him, people screaming, weapons clashing – was it a nightmare?

"Aue! Protect the children Lani," hissed his father, grabbing his spear. His mother shoved him and his two sisters behind her, eyes frantic with panic, as she craned to see what was happening. Her scream of anguish made them close their eyes tightly.

"No, no, no, please, this can't be happening!" Lani began to keen. Misery slid down her sorrow-ravaged face in fat droplets. His father was dead, Starboy was now the man of the house. His duty was to protect his family. Taking his father's whale-bone mere (striking club), he ran to the doorway, releasing his battle cry. The warriors were surprised to be attacked by such a small boy.

"I am Starboy! Last of the navigators, a son of the sea – die traitors!"

The warriors drew back. As seafarers, they were highly superstitious. Nobody wanted to kill a son of the sea.

"Take him," yelled their leader, "I want him unhurt. If he's navigator spawn, he can serve me." The chief of the raiders was consumed by lust for the boy's beautiful mother, perhaps she could give him fearless sons.

The village was overcome in minutes, by the enemy within. Men were slaughtered mercilessly, and the comeliest girls and women herded together.

"Lani, you have a brave son and no man. I will take you, and your family, into my home if you come quietly," said the chief.

"Will my son have a life?" She raised solemn eyes to the man who destroyed her world.

"Yes, he will be raised as one of my own." Lani inclined her head. She and her children gathered their belongings, numb with shock and grief. Starboy was seated with the warriors in the waka.

"Show me your skills young warrior, and I will spare your mother and sisters."

The ancestral knowledge of Starboy's lineage shone, he had already been initiated in the sacred sea-cave. His voyages with the raiders would take him throughout the Pacific and into manhood until his ocean father reclaimed him, and a mana wahine stole his heart.

*Wandering Writer - wrote a short story at the request of her nearest and dearest. Starman is a navigator and character in The Spirit Voyager Series. In Guardians of the Ancestors, he navigates first for marauding invaders and later for Marama and her people in their quest for a new home in Aotearoa. He is a complex but loveable character who survives a traumatic childhood which we get a glimpse of in this story.

Initiated by his grandfather as a son of the sea, Starman is the stuff that legends are made of. During the epic voyage to Aotearoa and in the company of Marama, his spiritual connections and the skills of generations of navigators come into play. Read more about the series at www.rdewolf.com.

Purakau Tipuna

Tipuna whispering
Weaving words
Taringa tune attentively
Mitochondrial murmurs
Echoes of past
Purakau - preserved lesson
Close to me now
In my blood
Flexing fingers coaxed
Story written
Brushed in strokes
Upon embracing canvas
Legacy
For future generations
Mine and yours, kuia
Taringa tune attentively
Woven words
Tipuna whispering

*Pencil Pusher - inspired by the brushstrokes and korero of a local artist. At an Arts Festival, she was lucky enough to hear the stories behind the paintings of some talented wahine which got her brain ticking and pencil twitching.

As the story unfolded, I was reminded of the power and continuity of our Maori oral storytelling tradition and I reflected on the stories passed down to me by my Nanny, Dad, Mum, and wonderful Aunties. In the story, there were common ancestry, cultural concepts, and connections that captivated me and transported me back to childhood and I heard my Tīpuna whispering in my ears.

You are never too old to enjoy a great story or find inspiration in the work of others.

I Am Titi

Puffinus griseus
Sooty Shearwater
Muttonbird
Titi

Some call me Chatham Island Chicken
That is where I'm from
Whatever you call me – I am too delicious for my own good

Cousin to the glamorous albatross, and petrel
I nest offshore, burrows made in remote places
The mainland is not for me – too many mouths to feed
Days at sea, nocturnal land visits
Find a squeeze in breeding season
If I'm lucky

Only ever one egg laid – don't scramble it
No replacements available
More than 50 days of incubating
Half the year gone with hatching and fledging
Oh the responsibility!

Blasted mammalian predators – give me the shits!
Wing north for warmth when it gets too cold

But my colony calls me - back to Rekohu
Always home...
Wrapped in fat
Packed in salt
I will die called Yum.

*Waxing Writer - The writer's mother loved her 'Chatham Island Chicken'. Muttonbirds would arrive at the house - fat, salty, and begging for a pot hook up with watercress or puha. Lydia Dawn, never lost her excitement or enthusiasm for the tasty muttonbird and the writer will never eat one without remembering her. Although it was the writer's Dad who made them look so terribly sweet as he licked his fingers, and he was horrified when his daughter did not like the rich fat, just the salty flesh.

Off to the shops with you, and get the pot on, or pull out your camera and travel to wild places to capture this darting bird - Titi.

Tinana - Body

Tinana
Broken into pieces
Ugly and mishappen
Gracious assembly
Beauty of form
Captivating pump
Bellows fed by Gods
Cleanser of crimson – myriad tasks
Nature's computer
Well of emotion
Sanctity of spirit
Stretching for creation
Aspiring to divinity
Tinana

*Internal Inking - Sometimes you just have to let yourself be amazed by the human body. When you look at our individual parts, well, most of them look kind of yuk. Picture an ear, or an arm even by itself without the rest of the body - not pretty.

But, you put it all together and you have the beauty of form and motion.

Besides our hard-working hands and feet, we also forget about our internal organs. So within the poem, I hope you appreciated the nod to our heart, liver, and that intriguing mystery - the brain.

There is so much we don't understand about ourselves. Our skin is special and we don't really get it at all, but it's the brain that drives our thoughts and emotions.

A toast to all our organs! Maybe with some water to keep the liver and kidneys feeling peachy.

Flax to Flax

By
Hand
Nature
Melded
Fibrous
Wonder
Strong
Supple
Trembling
In breeze
Whipping
Lashing gales
Strands scraped
And separated
Dried and dyed
Bleached colour
Crafted anew
Artistic expression
Flesh-hugging cloth
Enjoyment, usefulness
Adornment, warmth

Startling versatility
 No matter shape
  Assumed colour
   Or manipulation
    Remaking of you
   A desirable item
  Beautiful flax
 You are still flax
Never unmade
Always flax.

*Scribe Salute to the beauty of harakeke - flax. A natural and traditional resource that features prominently in the Maori world because it's so useful for making durable and beautiful items. The writer remembers her Nanny making kete (a woven bag with handles) to take to the beach and gather kaimoana (seafood) but you can also make rope, raurau (eating baskets), mats, clothing - let's face it that's where linen comes from - and beautiful artistic weaving to name a few uses.

The poem is also a metaphor for conquered, colonised, or dominated people throughout time who retain their shape, form, culture, and unique characteristics. While at times people can also be changed, manipulated, and transformed in all sorts of ways, the essence of who and what you are remains the same.

You are always flax.

Leila of the Light

A gift from Papatuanuku
Swaddled in aroha
Whakapapa, umbilically connected

Gunga-glow coals
Driftwood burned
Fire-lit, lustrous hair

Karanga of tide
Restless life churning
Ebb and flow with me?

Wairua, flaming hope
Flickering dance of potential
Shimmer of future

Grasp opportunities
Wring drops of goodness
Your place, your earth, your choices

Warmth of whanau

Lights the way
Arms of Whareponga await you.

*Literary Love - Poet missed the special occasion to be at home with her Mummy, but she was there in spirit and words to celebrate the coming of age of a special miss with flaming locks. Some people inspire the pen to drip poetry.

Hungry in Germany

Tot ziens Nederland
Doei!

Last stop roadhouse
Petrol, gas, food and WC
The sign oooozed promise

We left the motorway
Truck lured behind us
Greeted by potholes

Triumphant weeds – smugly rooting
Abandoned border control buildings
No longer employed with purpose

No fuel
No food
No toilet

Untrustworthy sign
Promise broken

Just like the road

Forty-five minutes
Speeding past German fields
Where have they hidden the food?

Driver gets a mint
Then another - instead of lunch

Parking and WC signs abound
What? No knife and fork

At last
The cutlery sign we've been searching for

Leave the motorway in a corkscrew of bitumen
Where is it?
We passed it
Scheiße! (shit!)

Turn around and go back
A roadside shop – with food
Hurrah!

Stocked with so many beers
Toys and cards
Pastries – but the cabinet is full of flies
Better get a sandwich from the closed display
And coffee ...mmm

We top up our supplies
Adding biscuits and crisps to mints and water
We won't go hungry again

Back on the road
Roadhouse stops and petrol everywhere
Scheiße! (shit!)

Only the first hour was a desert of nothing
Germany is a pantry of sustenance

But

Don't buy your petrol
In the highwaymen's den
No prices displayed
Forty-four Euro cents
More per litre
Then in town
Merde... (shit!)

*Wandering Writer got a bit hungry in Germany - hence the title. Traveling from the Netherlands to Denmark by car offers a nice opportunity to stay in the beachside town of Heilligen-hafen and catch the ferry from Puttgarden. But, it had been years since the writer traveled this way and she forgot that when you leave the Netherlands there is nothing along the highway for ages - and nothing had changed.

Enter hangry driver who has to do all the driving because

the writer doesn't enjoy driving on the 'other' side of the road, and should have eaten more breakfast. Godverdomme! (god-dammit!) Now everyone is starving and there is not a single crossed cutlery sign in sight. Germany has gone all New Zealand, and only has picnic tables and truck stops.

There is never a trip to Germany without a petrol drama either and the prices on the side of the motorway are eye-watering - ouch!

The autobahn has also been consigned to the past and there are now speed limits. So, to the angry young road-rage man, who was annoyed with Wandering Writer and co. for doing the 120 km speed limit while passing a truck - she hopes your life gets better.

The Good, the Gold &
the Greed

Wedding band glinting
Star-birthed gold
Reflection
Shiny mirror of tears

Grandma's originally
Memories
Years passed by

Dug from ground
Machinery tearing
Voracious talons seeking

Consideration?
Not a drop

Scarred earth
Festering sores
The precious

A treasure
Valued keepsake, well worn
Origin and whakapapa – lost
Blazing beginning buried

Gobbled
By greed

*Blazing Brand - Gold, created in the birthing of stars. Rare, valuable, and beautiful in its polished, glinting finery. Poet was intrigued by the origin of gold and eyes lit with imaginary starbursts eons past.

The flip side of all that beauty is the ugliness of our scarred earth mother and the destruction of civilisations in pursuit of the riches gold delivers.

Poetry on a see-saw for the writer in this outing of the pen.

Leaving the Nest

It took some time
For me to leave the nest
I enjoy a sheltered life
But it's probably for the best

Don't know how it happened
Somehow, I'm in mid-twenties
The cuddly toys are gone
Honestly, I miss them plenty

But life beckons
Crooks a coaxing finger at the door
No longer can I ignore it
By humming and gazing at the floor

Off once more to study
This time in another city
Not too far hurrah
Parents roll eyes in self-pity

Falling on my feet

I get an awesome pad
Try to burn it with the microwave
But then so does my Dad

Great Aunt gives me a couch
It's actually quite posh
Not a student pad at all
And doesn't cost lots of dosh

So now I'm independent
With my own sweet place
But I go home every weekend
To hang out with my mates

I do socialise where I live
But I like my group of friends
And I sneak home quietly
Do some shopping, make amends

One day I'll meet a partner
Guess we'll get our own place then
Until I really have to lovely parents
I return to my childhood den.

*Contemplative Chronicler - warns parents to send their children to study in a city far away. Why? Because the lure of free food, comfort, and familiarity is like a drug to some children and students. If they can train, drive or bus home they are like friggin' boomerangs. Overseas universities and tertiary institutions are highly recommended for 'apron string' severing.

Screwed Up

Screwed up

Discarded in the bin of unwanted

Don't make people feel like your pie packet

To be taken away in the wheelie bin

The paper was once a tree

Living...
Breathing...
Cleansing...
Our world.

*Penned Perspective - Yes, the poem has an environmentally literal message - let's be honest, humans waste, waste, waste, and make mess, mess, mess - ugh.

The poem is also about people. Everyone comes into the world with a clean slate, completely innocent. Issues arise when you can't 'tick the box' society and bureaucracy want you to tick. No fixed address, no bank account, no identification, no computer or phone literacy, no qualifications, no referees, or no money, and you are assigned the value of the pie packet.

Is humanity losing it? - the humanity I mean. Did we swap caring and valuing life for a bunch of paperwork and tick-boxes? Poet has led a good life, but whenever she enters the world of people less fortunate or marginalised, she despairs that society has created a Bureaucracy Monster - Goliath, for people to battle. To quote my Dad 'it's like pushing shit uphill with a blunt stick.' For the many Davids out there who battle the Goliath every day for others, the pen hails you as the heroes and champions you are.

Herbaceous Life - Racked with Spice

AN ESSAY - SACRE BLEU!

Why are we so obsessed with food and slaves to our flavour cravings - why I ask myself?

Chefs purposefully engage all senses to create memorable dining experiences, but two play pivotal roles. Taste and smell have their own biology as both react to chemicals in food, and the oral and nasal cavities are directly connected, linking them closely. When they work together to identify chemicals in food or drink, we develop what we know as flavour. Flavour is a sensation that uses many senses at once — an amalgam of taste, texture, temperature, and smell of what we are eating.[1]

I believe the sisterhood between taste and smell, tongue and nose, is as inseparable as twins. Neuroscience agrees with me.

Studies have found a connection between odours and powerful memories. Scientists believe the anatomy of the brain allows olfactory signals to get to the limbic system very quickly. Experts say the memories associated with smells tend to be older and thought about less often, meaning the recollection is very vivid when it happens.[2]

No surprise then that some of my strongest early memories are of food. The fragrance and flavour of thyme transport me to the ghost of Christmas past. My mother bustled in the kitchen, preparing stuffing with the stale bread we rubbed until it filled a large enamel tub with the finest crumbs. "Are we done yet?" I would ask, hopefully. Invariably, the answer was "no, not ready yet," and we would continue to combat the lumpy bread. However, the smell of Mum's softly sauteed onions in butter, salt, pepper, and mixed herbs from the packet would greet us, but the piéce de résistance was thyme from the garden. A herbaceous invitation for my stomach to rumble in applause. The weird part is I enjoyed tasting the mixture, but I don't eat stuffing. Unlike Clinton, I love to inhale, and perhaps the quote below explains the strength of taste recall.

'A functional link between the brain region responsible for taste memory and the area responsible for encoding the time and place we experienced the taste had been found. The findings expose the complexity and richness of the simple sensory experiences that are engraved in our brains and that in most cases we aren't even aware of.'[3]

My life, although sometimes sweet, is mostly savoury - liberally salted with tasty plates, peppered with mishaps, occasional hot chilli happenings and merrily infused with travel. When did my love affair with herbs and spices begin? Certainly not with the tough curly parsley growing in our veggie garden, that greened Mum's cauliflower and white sauce. I promise not to stray into the overpowering smell and taste of dreaded cauliflower, which I still loathe.

In 1987 I flew to London. After it rained for two weeks, I gave up waiting for it to stop and brought a Eurail pass. The afternoon before a hurricane hit, I jumped on a train and headed to Nice with two newly acquired Northern American mates. Our first taste of freshly baked French croissant was sublime - light, flaky pastries, unlike anything we'd tasted before. They flirted like Cancan dancers' skirts through our mouths in a teasing procession. The staff laughed at our hasty repeat visits as we overindulged in gluttonous glee. In all fairness, we later hiked for miles, with our backpacks up a hill, to get to the Youth Hostel, so our calorific pétit dejeuner was warranted.

France, Italy, Greece and Spain ignited a passion for food. Whether it was a baguette patiently proved, a Margherita pizza aromatic with basil, Greek salad with olive oil, herbs and vinegar or tapas laced with garlic – I loved it. The spicy herb-tinged air of the Greek Islands still captivates my nostrils. It reminds me of the rosemary, thyme and clover honey I drizzle on my fruit and yoghurt in the morning or the aromatic waft of bay leaf and nutmeg that fills the taverna when moussaka comes out of the oven. The memories of tastes and smells convince me that Europe coaxed my incubating 'foodie' out of hibernation.

A vegetarian at the time, when I returned in the winter, the food on a budget in London was awful. There are only so many Ploughman's and cooked breakfasts with beans you can eat before one's tiny nose wrinkled in displeasure. Then the heavens opened, and angels began to sing because when I started working at the YHA Youth Hostel, my new flatmate Deb cooked wonderfully. She also introduced me to the joys of Indian cuisine, which endures as a firm favourite. Weaned off my backpacker diet of bread, fruit, cheese and biscuits, I dived into the tantalising masala of spice world with the gusto of a pig in mud. Perhaps my enthusiasm was inflamed by the fact I enjoyed eating again because it was affordable. It wasn't long before I looked forward to a curry on the way home from the Pub, even though I didn't drink. Deb learned to cook authentic Bengali dishes from a friend at university and shared a wicked chickpea and potato curry recipe, which I can make with most vegetables – bliss!

After my three-month holiday in Europe morphed into three years and a new career, I reluctantly returned to Australia. On the way home, I stopped in Bangkok. Thailand is the only country I have ever visited where I ate six times a day and lost weight. The food is divine. Cooks prepare perfect portions in laze-inducing heat, as delicately balanced flavours harmonise with the palate. So, I embarked on a holiday fling with lemongrass, coriander, lime, ginger and chilli. I may have indulged in some sweet chunks of freshly cut pineapple on the side, such a bargain from the street vendors. The introduction to southeast Asian food fired my appetite to sample the delights awaiting me in Sydney and laid the groundwork for an appreciation of Vietnamese, Indonesian, Thai and fusion cuisine.

After such tasty adventures, I wondered what I would rack up next. Never one to rest on my laurels, or bay leaves, I shacked up with a trained chef's toothbrush, towel and suitcase and later made an honest man out of him. Our culinary adventures together are legendary. Everything from dining at Tetsuya's to eating freshly caught tuna dipped in seawater off the back of a boat in Aitutaki. We ate all of the emblems on the Australian coat of arms while living in Cairns, along with crocodile, snake and some lovely lemony green ants, which are an excellent bush source of vitamin C. I promise we harmed no koalas in the writing of this essay, and I must say they make eucalyptus leaves look yummy, although I don't find their medicinal smell appealing.

In the food Olympics, I have two claims to fame. Eating oysters from the shell is a well-honed skill I cultivated in New Zealand from childhood. The French hostel staff in La Rochelle were astounded by my prowess as I appreciatively hoovered up dozens of the salty bivalves. I ate everything left over on tasting night, delighting my hosts. Sea-flavoured slimy textured oysters are a love or hate relationship – for me, l'amour.

I shared the second podium-earning eating performance with the man I married. We once finished a 15-course Lebanese banquet at a favourite restaurant in Surry Hills, Sydney. What a procession of flavour bombs that meal was. It started with olives, pickled chilli, hummus, babaganoush, tabouli, pita bread, falafel, stuffed vine leaves, kibbeh, beans in tomato, chicken shish with white garlic, lamb kebabs with yoghurt sauce, baklava, Turkish delight and Lebanese coffee. Who knows why we were so hungry that day? The staff were so shocked that they came out of the kitchen to offer us more dessert. To be fair, we were never able to eat the lot again – although we delighted in trying because the garlicky, char, and smoke flavours tempted us often. When we arrived on the Lycian coast of Turkey to sample the complex spices of the Ottoman Empire, our tastebuds were finely tuned.

In conclusion, I concur with the scientists' claim that taste, smell and memory speak to one another because the memories inspired by flavour are incredibly vivid. Taste is thought to be centred in the brain's insular cortex and represents experience from inside our bodies, not externally like our other senses. There is also a theory that taste and flavour signal the nutrients our body needs.[4]

Science aside, my life in flavour is a well-travelled smorgasbord of colourful, tasty experiences - herbaceous and racked with spice, with a tiny sprinkle of nerdy curiosity.

[1]https://www.brainfacts.org/thinking-sensing-and-behaving/learning-and-memory/2015/taste-and-memory

[2]https://www.verywellmind.com/why-do-we-associate-memories-so-strongly-with-specific-smells-5203963#:~:text=Scientists%20believe%20that%20smell%20and,very%20vivid%20when%20it%20happens.

[3]https://www.sciencedaily.com/releases/2014/09/140922110149.htm

[4]https://news.cornell.edu/stories/2019/03/sweet-spot-research-locates-taste-center-brain

*Studious Scribbler decided to participate in an essay competition. The topic was food and flavour and she promised to participate, even though she hadn't written an essay since leaving school. Blowing off the cobwebs, Poet and Fiction Author revisits on google what an essay is and how it's constructed, giving herself a pat on the back for using one of the 'R's Research. She's a foodie and as the topic salivated out of her pen, the writer recalled the flavours of home and travelling to many places.

The scientific relationship between taste and smell in relation to flavour was particularly intriguing and scribbler indulged her 'nerdy nerd' with fact-finding tasty titbits. While this essay wasn't a winner, it gives a glimpse into the writer's brain and puku - stomach.

Ella Moray

Ella
Sitting alone
Innocent, vulnerable – beautiful
And sweet

Tanned and leggy
We couldn't leave you
To travel alone
From Roma Central Station

"It's not safe, the ride to Brindisi."
"Travel with us for a while."
Has ever Roma Station been lit
By such a high-voltage smile

Two Aussies, a Kiwi, and our new
Danish-English friend
Little did we know it would be
A friendship without end

Sunbaked atop the Acropolis

Onto a ferry island bound
Hypnotic inky swell of sea
Helios kissed so young and free

Aussies were headed to Ios
So, we tagged along
To the party island soaked in sun
Cocktails, dance, and song

We danced among ancient ruins
Under starlit sky
Went early, got our drinks for free
Because we danced for joy you and I

Sunshine, beach and sand
Yoghurt, honey, Greek toast every day
Drank too much but we tanned
Lazy days passing but on we did play

Then one day you confessed
"I should be starting school"
I bought you a ticket home
Father reported you, a missing person to Interpol!

But that wasn't the end of that story
At the church I met your mother
Burdened with grief, the loss of your light
We held fast to one another

"Thank you" said Erkel

"For saving Ella when she was young"
"Not a problem, I'm sorry you worried
While we endlessly had good fun."

Mor told me they called the hospitals
And your photo was on Greek TV
A missing person – disappeared
The culprit, youth frolics not tragedy

So, my darling Ella
Downplayed the situation you see
She knew I'd feel guilty
That we'd partied on with glee

We shared this story at the wake
It made family and friends smile
I felt your angelic laughter Ella
As you fluttered your wings in style

Holding the missing pieces
Of life's puzzle that was yours
I hold you in my heart of hearts
As you play to rapturous applause.

*Poignant Poetry - The poet shed buckets of tears when she lost her darling friend. Ella was mourned by many including her international friends and fellow writers and poets. Fortunately, Poet and Hubby were able to travel to Copenhagen, and celebrate Ella's magical life with her family and friends.

The love of life is a gift and Ella Moray Williams was clever enough to make the most of her life. The poet recalls the magnitude of her smile, the enduring feeling that she should protect her, and the bottomless well of friendship maintained with letters, postcards, phone calls, emails, and zooms, shared over almost 35 years.

Ella Moray dances on in her music, her poetry, but most of all - her two gorgeous children.

Binary Star Love

ETERNITY TOGETHER

From here, a single object
Viewed with naked eye
Bound to orbit one another
Sparkling jewels in night sky

Falling, falling, fallen
Shooting stars in our eyes
Love's captives, unaware
Future yet unrealised

You drifted in,
Attracted by the gravity field
Locked in place
Circling, magnetic appeal

When I pushed you pulled,
And same in reverse
We stepped out a tango
For this day, we rehearsed

Then the question was popped
Shining star on a band
Shall we dance for eternity?
One woman for one man

And now, when the day
Bids the moon 'take my place'
We share news, nourish bodies
Nurture souls and hold space

Do the dishes, let in dogs
We collapse with a slouch
TV banter, tired, cuddle-up
Fall asleep on the couch

Families in life's blender
Lives intertwined
Children and grand kids
Gently mellowed, finest wine

There are horses and a cat
Abundant, fur-babies galore
And an orchard of avocados
Just in case we get bored

Our vibrant, full lives
Amalgamated so well
Laughter, fun and magic

Cast such a potent spell

The twinkle of your eyes
The warmth of your smile
Make me want to be with you
Take my hand, stay awhile

His and hers gumboots
Parked by our door
Shared home, open hearts
How could one ask for more?

Stay with me forever,
My darling, binary star
Grow old, heaven's union,
Witnessed from afar

I am yours, you are mine
Everything in life
Partners, a pair
A husband and wife.

*Romantic Ruminations - When the Poet's bestie from primary school, Paula Heney, asked her to do a reading or a poem at her wedding, out came the pencil. Why not write a poem for the happy couple, she thought? Although poetry has been written about love through the ages, each love has its own unique story.

After seeing the binary stars of Alpha Centauri through

a telescope, the poet cataloged them and their relationship to each other and filed them away for future material. There is something enduring and romantic about the binding together of two entities in the heavens.

It's a special honour and privilege to be able to create work for people you love, and the Poet was tickled pink. Thanks to Paula and Ross Savage for inspiring a love poem for their big day. True love isn't easy to find, and when it comes along it's time for a major celebration.

Hark, do we hear the popping of champagne corks? Time to go... Bubbles o'clock.

Almost Grown

Graduated – yes!
Phew what a relief
At times I wasn't sure
But I restored my self-belief

Off I went, to employment land
Internship, all gung ho
Hone my craft and trade
Quite a lot I don't know

I traveled by myself
Made me nervous without the fam
Who normally sorts out everything
From home to Gdansk

The sweet smell of money
Landing in my pocket
Hours perusing pages
To spend it like a rocket

And when you're feeling blue

Just buy a few good beers
Even if you are happy
There's someone to wish you cheers

Learn to do my laundry
Make my bed without my mummy
Thank goodness for the cook
To look after hungry tummy

When I finally go home
So grown up and alone
Someone comes to get me
And working bestie - trusty phone

Bedroom like I left it
Except, smells nice and it's clean
Did you touch my stuff?
Like a toddler vent my spleen

For while I'm almost grown up
I haven't yet left the nest
It's so cosy and – well nice
Deep down I know I'm blessed

But as I grow older
My drunkenness is less amusing
Sleeping on the couch and making mess
After steady alcohol abusing

Every now and then

Mum does want to kick me out
Eventually, I'll have to go
Cause sometimes I'm a lout

Still, the food is great
The rent so jolly cheap
And I feel safe at home
When I lay my head to sleep

One day I'll have some kids
Geez I hope they aren't like me
They will drive me round the bend
And live at home eternally.

*Pithy Poet - empathises with parents whose kids live at home...forever. Well, it may or may not be forever but there will be moments when it feels like it. The trouble for kids is that your relationship doesn't change with your parents until you have lived as an adult and understand little things like buying toilet paper, changing the loo roll, buying food at the supermarket, cooking, paying bills, or - cleaning. Kids realise shampoo and soap don't just appear in the shower and the salt & pepper shaker aren't self-replenishing. These are the kind of steps you take from childhood to being a real grown-up. Don't worry Mums and Dads, there will come a time when they want to be free or you give them a little shove to launch them.

Poet, like many Mums and Dads, couldn't wait to leave home and become independent - what has changed she wonders?

Ocean of Sunset

Ocean of Sunset
Floral cartwheel
Paradise explored
To bravely go
Where no woman has gone before
Dive into my calm
Pool of creation
Sootheness of soul
Mirimiri of mauri
Sail with me
Matariki karanga
Restless cells
Yearning for stars
Waka exploring, endless possibilities.

*Sentimental Scribbler - Now and then the scribbler goes to see different art. The piece was inspired by moving graphic art that enthralled and amused her - bravo to the artist whose imagination travelled oceans of water and space.

Poutokomanawa

Feet firm
Reaching for Ranginui
Planted on Papatuanuku
Connecting earth and sky
I am you
You are a piece of me
Watching over us
Guardian, of your ancestors
Light, in our whare
Shining the way
Heart of hearts
Silent sentinel
Staunch bearing
Seeing all
No judgment speaking
Centre of home
Well of warmth
Chosen
Binding together
Poutokomanawa

*Poetic Prompting - When the poet was given the prompt Poutokomanawa, she embarked on some research. Not just what the word means in Uncle George's dictionary, but the essence of Poutokomanawa, and in a personal way, what it means and how it makes the poet feel. The shape emerged from the words and memories of the heart of wharenui.

Finding Mokopuna

A WORD SEARCH GAME

*Riddly Ridiculous Writing - The Writer has included the names of many mokopuna in the text - some words or names may be spelled a little differently and some names are in tricky places across multiple words. Can you find them all?

Georgia, Nutty, Dylan, Hamuera, Cassiopeia, Kura, Doonie, Sky, Winiata, Lily, Blaze, Jai, Kyana, Waikohu, Te Ao, Pourewa, Dakeyrus, Gavin, Vorei, Charlie, Walter, Armani, Blaine, Dina, Kalladin, Harlem, Haami, Materoa, Whitireia, Kimura, Finley, Darcy, Walker, Kairo, Manatu, Piripono, Teana, Manawa

On a trip to Harlem, New York not the Netherlands, Pourewa (Po) asked her cousin if they could have a look at the old jail. Well, the sky was blue so her mate roared an enthusiastic 'yes' in response, looking forward to a stroll. But, it wasn't easy to find, harder than to locate Aorangi, wrestle a buffalo or search for Cassiopeia in the night sky. Hamuera paused then taking Po's arm, an idyll man loitering on the street asked if they were lost.

"What's your name?" asked Hamuera.

"Kim Uranski, at your service," the man replied. He turned out to be the most helpful man and gave them detailed instructions on how to find the jail. "When you get there, ask for my mate Fin Leyland, he's a tour guide and I'll text him you Maori people are coming. He'll be well excited, he loves rugby and the haka. Say, how did you come to be in New York buddy?"

"We did win iata plane tickets in a raffle - cool aye."

"Well ain't that something."

The sun was so hot by the time the kids arrived at the Jail, their skin was ablaze.

"Uh oh, mack, ur, ain't gonna be happy," Hamuera said in his best New Yorker accent. Pourewa dissolved in stitches.

"Walk er, down the sidewalk buddy. Whaddaya waitin' for," she replied.

Old posters were plastered on the outside of the jail advertising everyone from the Rolling Stones, to Darcy Bussell.

"Man this is sick, Allidan probably couldn't open sesame his way in here," said Hamuera.

They purchased their tickets all excited and the girl at the ticket booth, Blaine was her name, and she asked "Have you read Lorna Doon" i.e. she wanted to discuss books with Hamuera.

"Oh man, away we go Po, didn't think we would find a hunting carnivor either in New York," he muttered under his breath.

"Take da key rascal, maybe grab my phone number later" winked Blaine.

"Ha, amicable girl that Blaine," said Po.

"I'd rather phone a hungry desperate anaconda," he laughed.

Fin met them with her husky Ana. "I also have another husky Koh but he's hiding, take a look behind the piano, the Kawai, Koh under there?" she asked.

They stopped to buy ice cream and tried pistachio which had a creamy nutty flavour, even better than the peanut ice-cream in Georgia, and the passionfruit yoghurt ice in Pasadina. They did the tour with Fin, which was awesome, and afterwards he took them to the deli. He ordered them the sauerkraut, chicken piripiri pon oatbread, so they ate their kai rolling their eyes because it was so good. Fin asked them to choose a drink they hadn't tried before.

"Hey man a tumeric chai, that sounds awesome," said Hamuera.

"Hibiscus and waterlily yoghurt smoothie for me," said Po, "this is better than going to Whakarewarewa!"

The waitress shot them a look, "no shoddy language in my deli," she waggled her finger teasing.

"It's not bad language miss, it's a Maori place name and they have boiling mud there," giggled Hamuera.

'Oh heavens, that sounds exciting," said the waitress.

"My cousin Whitireia is a star in the heavens," said Hamuera.

"You don't say. My Dad Charlie and his brother Walter are up there too."

"Wow, my little twin brothers are named after my Papa Charlie and Walter, and Uncle Takawai – that's so mean!" said Po.

"You don't say. Fin Leyland, you and your little friends can have your food on the house. They were meant to come here, full'o chutzpah. I feel really close to my Dad and Uncle right now. Gavin, make 'em my special, a pastrami on rye," she shouted to the cook, wiping a tear from her eye.

"OMG! I have a brother called Gavin," squealed Po.

"Get outta town," said the waitress shaking her head "ain't that the darnedest thing ever. I want you guys and your family to come eat with my family. My sister owns one of the best Pizza joints in New York."

They nodded, excited as they munched their food and messaged the rest of the family the good news.

This just goes to show, there are huskies and good people everywhere.

*In Poetry In a Pear Tree, Miss Finley was so excited to find her name inside, she asked the poet for a copy, then if she could be in this book as well. There is nothing like growing your fan base when they are young so the poet thought - why not? It was such a good idea, that it metamorphosised into a story and a game with mokopuna names.

In special memory of Nanny Ruby Reedy, who loved all her mokopuna so dearly. A joy and privilege for the poet to share mokopuna with such an outstanding and loving role model.

Thanks

The Rhythmic Weave dream team strikes again! While the production team this year is me, me and me - Te Tairawhiti is full of creative inspiring human beings who fill the world with colour and inspiration.

It has been a busy year with Tairawhiti Writers Hub producing the second local anthology, but the reading and editing process fills me with wonder about people's talents - thank you, and congratulations to the 40 writers published in 2022. Thanks, Charlie Holland for organising a new group format, Taranga Kent for your input, and Gillian Moon for your on-going mahi - you are also wonderful friends.

Tairawhiti Technology Trust Writing Group - what a writing whanau we are! Polly and Barney Crawford, Katrina Reedy, Molly Pardoe, Benita Kape, Paddy Noble, Suzanne Pinfold, Claire Morgan, Allison Namana, La, Kristin (our boomerang returned), PP, Alice, Moana, and all the attendees who have popped into the Hub this year - you are fantastic and I've been grateful for your support as a writer and in life for the aroha you give - losing Rodney Baker was hard for us all. Makere Wanoa, congratulations on producing your first book, it was challenging but you did it - ka pai.

Renay Charteris, Cain Kerehoma, Mariska van Galen, Seda, Stef, Josh and the crew at Taiki E! - last year I called you out for your positivity and community mahi and you just continue to amp it up. Loved the Escape Room and Startup weekend with you guys again. Keep changing the world - you inspire me.

Thank you to everyone who supported me and Ieme through losing our Mum and a dear friend in quick succession and especially our Frisian whanau HJ, Tineke, Foeke, and Tjerk for putting us up when I was too sick to go anywhere. Mum and Dad de Wolf - Foeke and Corrie - we are grateful for your longevity and love. Whanau and friends who are always there with a kind word, a cuddle, or a message when the going gets tough - you know who you are!

To Paula and Ross, Wihi and Cody congratulations and thanks for getting married because we needed some weddings after the funerals, and more than one makes me feel like we are winning.

The last helping at my gratitude buffet is always reserved for my husband, Ieme de Wolf, who listens to me talking to my computer and having the occasional rant when things aren't going right.

Acknowledgments

Astro Tours John Drummond
https://gisborneastrotours.com
William Shakespeare
https://en.wikipedia.org/wiki/William_Shakespeare
Barrett Browning
https://en.wikipedia.org/wiki/Elizabeth_Barrett_Browning
Pablo Neruda
https://en.wikipedia.org/wiki/Pablo_Neruda
Cardi B
https://www.cardibofficial.com
Tairawhiti Writers Hub
https://tairawhitiwrite.wordpress.com
Tairawhiti Technology Trust
https://www.taitech.nz
Taiki E! Impact House
https://www.taikie.nz

Brothers In Whalesong

COMING SOON

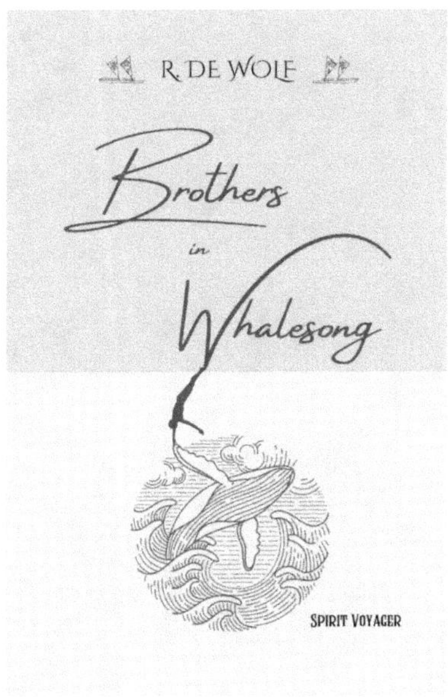

Book Three of the Spirit Voyager Series

Kai bonded with whale Ira, in the womb of his mother Marama, but he's also a son of the sea descended from an illustrious line of navigators. When Tangaroa sets Kai and Ira a task, they answer the call to voyage, where adventure and danger await them.

About the Author

R de Wolf was born Regina Ngarimu on the East Coast of
New Zealand and is of Maori descent. She moved around
with her family starting school in Reporoa, before returning
to the family home, Pohatukura, to live with Nanny Maraea
and attend Manutahi School. 1977 saw the Ngarimu clan re-
locate to the Bay of Plenty and Regina started school at Ohope
Primary School, then went on to Whakatane Intermediate and
Trident High School. After leaving New Zealand for her OE,
she lived worked, and studied overseas for 29 years, before

returning to New Zealand in 2014. Currently, she resides in sunny Turanganui-a-Kiwa - Gisborne with her husband. The call to write came home with her.

In 2020 R. de Wolf published her debut fiction novel, Guardians of the Ancestors - Book One of the Spirit Voyager Series, and short story Crushed Violet, in Kaituhi Rawhiti – A Celebration of East Coast Writers. In 2021 The Future Weavers - Book Two launched in November, and a book of poems, Poetry In a Pear Tree, was published in December.

De Wolf writes about the issues she is passionate about – equality, women's rights, the balance of nature, and the spiritual connection to our ancestors and place. A self-confessed nerd and Sci-Fi fan, The Goodness Algorithm was R. de Wolf's first dystopian novel where she ventures into leadership, politics, and difficult choices for humanity, posing questions to the reader. Brothers in Whalesong - Book Three will be ready for subscribers by Christmas and hit the shelves next year. It's been a busy year for de Wolf who co-edited and co-produced East Coast Anthology Kaituhi Rāwhiti Two - Weaving of Words with Gillian Moon and Christopher McMaster. The volume includes diverse work from 40 writers at all stages of their writing careers and represents the spirit of a community-driven project powered by volunteers.

Poetry In a Pohutukawa is her second poetic effort, with accompanying reflections. Pohutukawa has a couple of stories as well as poems and, like the Pear Tree, was produced to entertain friends and family.

9 781991 189615